at first it felt like flying

Charlie Baylis & Andrew Taylor

Indigo Dreams Publishing

First Edition: at first it felt like flying
First published in Great Britain in 2019 by:
Indigo Dreams Publishing
24, Forest Houses
Halwill
Beaworthy
Devon
EX21 5UU

www.indigodreams.co.uk

Charlie Baylis & Andrew Taylor have asserted their right under the Copyright, Designs and Patents Act 1988 to be identified as the authors of this work.
©2019 Charlie Baylis & Andrew Taylor

ISBN 978-1-910834-99-2

British Library Cataloguing in Publication Data. A CIP record for this book can be obtained from the British Library.

This book is sold subject to the condition that it shall not, by way of trade or otherwise, be lent, re-sold, hired out, or otherwise circulated without the author's and publisher's prior consent in any form of binding or cover other than that in which it is published and without a similar condition including this condition being imposed on the subsequent purchaser.

Designed and typeset in Palatino Linotype by Indigo Dreams.
Cover artwork by Ronnie Goodyer at Indigo Dreams.

Printed and bound in Great Britain by 4edge Ltd.
www.4edge.co.uk

Papers used by Indigo Dreams are recyclable products made from wood grown in sustainable forests following the guidance of the Forest Stewardship Council.

for

Nichola, Alex and Rachel
(AT)

and

Mary Elizabeth Baylis
(CB)

CONTENTS

juno 9

jaako 10

julianna 11

jabari 12

jenny 13

rebecca 14

ruby 15

rihanna 16

rachael 17

rebecca ii 18

jaime 20

jace 21

jacaranda 22

jandek 23

rose 24

rasputin 25

rupert 26

roland 27

rose ii 28

at first it felt like flying

juno

skirts around the tomato plants
before pinching out   Kevin showed
her the way

On the gravel drive a shape is left
when a car departs   It's easy to
count individual stones

Juno plays the stereo loudly
she says it helps   the tomatoes
especially when it rains

jaako

Say hi once in a while
spin the daisy

the street is a set
clouds are coal bags

Jaako roams the roofs
like the marten in Gourge

to the ornate sound
of harpsichords

recorded on cassette

julianna

Christmas Eve early
morning routine
a marine lake walk
Julianna's recording
a playlist playing

A few days on the island
new disc explored as she
sleeps along the coast road
the river gap shore lights at dusk

jabari

avoid Dr Google the meds
are expensive though melatonin
is relatively cheap

imported tea is good as are
car parts track the delivery
Gatwick – Heathrow – Brussels

Paris – Nantes and onwards behind
shutters a modern psychedelic
masterpiece 'Hello Nick'

jenny

is a friend of Alex who enjoyed
the fact that a Killers ticket was
sold at face value for an intimate

show where a bra was thrown
at the stage the US has eyes for
Venezuela's oil well there's a surprise

the train didn't go to Vegas we took
it to San Francisco the room was
strewn with fliers from Liverpool

rebecca

is a comet   she collides with a poem
about the realist movement in italian cinema
i get it   i think there were many great films

rebecca tastes of the beach at midnight   i
watch wave by wave wave by in the blue of her eyes
i lick her legs   rebecca is not a comet

rebecca works in a sweet shop   drips acid
onto reels   her passion for pearl is peach   she says
pistachio always tastes like the moon

ruby

paints my room chilli pepper red   flicks
raindrops from her lashes   undresses the language
of her tongue   hoarfrost and diphthong

angelic simulacrum   shooting stars   shoot the chute
of her neck   waterfalls   we saw as   waterfalls
were ruby's wet back from the ocean

were ruby's wet shoulders from the ocean   i
examine the movies in ruby's lip gloss   when we kiss
i can't stop thinking how blue the sky is

rihanna

rihanna holds up the sweetshop   chews her finger
off   waiting for the light to leave
every chink in the iceberg   she takes

my heart   my keys   my patience   leans on
my car   her silver hair   tumbles like starfall down a glacier
her naked body   shimmers from billboards

in the summer heat   *nobody touches her but the righteous*
nobody texts her in a crisis   my watch
explodes   i don't get it   the sky is no longer blue

rachael

i see her in the distance
weighing the trees   their scales
searching for that found sound

like a ship gliding serenely into an iceberg
mouth full of cloud   oceans'   impending
doom   rachael throws a sparrow into space   speaks

i need silence   don't touch me
those words were six of her words
the rest just sail away

rebecca ii

i'll never get tired of plucking pearls
from her peach mountain
the holes we dug which led

to las vegas   where a bra was thrown
at the stage   the titanic sails at twelve   the nylon dyes
amber shade   waves like the waves which waved

by in the blue of her eye   or the sunlight tipping
through grand cathedral windows
rolling an r and a j onto the scrabble board

jabez

When the laptop bag snaps in
the lock of the boot rush straight

to the out of town shopping area
and buy a new one

or when the lanterns blow in
the breeze cloud cover will follow

ensure that the washing is aired
and folded neatly in preparation

for ironing

jaime

picks the Xanax up for   after the shoot
the desert listening party with the silver
trailer   was broadcast live even advertised
in *The New York Times*

the Clubmasters have   a certain shine
certainly after cracking the Twitter code
sucking on sugared almonds and listening

to *Tomorrow's Harvest* at dusk put the phone
away after three songs

jace

autocorrects to Kace
as in Kace Face or Ace Face

on the A83 two lanes
into one causes difficulties

Proper tea is hard to come by
the milk has to be fresh

The 6.30 am New York to Rome
flight is late

it's nearly time to eat

jacaranda

cosy & casual   origins in coffee
the espresso machine was an innovation

beans on toast & Coca-Cola as payment

south of the equator   carpet seems
unnecessary 49 species to choose from

like lavender mist the eye is drawn to horizons

a cello melody   piano refrain
sequencing is a part like hand movement

jandek
i.m. Tom Raworth

Where can we go when we retire?
which hold me down by my head?

experience perhaps
shooting along (alone)
stockings because the word means what comes to mind
and turn
time: art is beamed to those antenna education should tune
rumours of the present (any present) then *deja vu* is a true
doppler effect

rose

13 meters and you should see her   the ghost
ship   14   we're here
the pictures clear   rose unravels in jack's

fingers   truth without logic   freud on fantasy
the atlantic gleaming from every port-hole   tinted rose
by the sunset   tinted rose by rose   on the couch

clothes off   everything a well brought up girl should be
angels flying out of her arse   five hundred invitations
mailed   "if you jump   i'll jump with you"

rasputin

the itch hits a glitch
blues shades wrap around my sunglasses   i miss
take   a hymn for the wind i live

in a moonlit laundrette under the sea
where there are many tails in the water
tails like who sucked off who in the cinema   tails of realism

with the name spelt clever like the ella in umbrella   *(ella*
ella)   sperm   the product of mimesis   watch this space
as it splits   below you   above you   beyond you

rupert
for rupert loydell

these new paradigms   crickets snogging
in summer rain   the graceful merlin
lands   in rose's hands   wholes open to ocean

the message on my t-shirt reads *this is the message*
on my t-shirt   glass rapping outside the tissue box
graffiti sprayed in french   *your mother sucks bears*

rupert   what can we do about this sinking ship?
how many copies of the solex brothers have you sold?
how much do i owe you for lunch?

roland

maybe you wont find a better dandelion
      nineteen down   than the one you lost
           roland drowns rebecca in an infinity pool
                says it might be better to just let it go

rihanna's growling eyes   killer whales killing poets
      rupert's iona loneliness   in the north atlantic
         rose and jack safe on the iceberg   mystery light
             bouncing from my car   the letter r i get it

               in   craters of full of rubies   'hi nick'

rose ii

jack   this is where we met
at first it felt like flying
my heart was pounding the whole time

jack put your hands on me
when the ship docks   i'm getting off with you
and   if you jump   i jump

immaculate bastards   mathematical certainty
raw money   hardened by china   in the sweetshop glow
i have seen an iceberg   i have seen an iceberg in your eyes

notes and acknowledgements:

thanks to the editors where versions of the following poems originally appeared:

rebecca — the new statesman
rebecca ii — lotus eater
ruby — zin daily
rihanna — the welter journal
rachael — the cadaverine
rose ii — ink sweat and tears
juno, julianna, jace, jacaranda and jaako — stride

rihanna contains elements of her song 'work' ft. drake

rose and rose ii were collaged from the script of 'titanic' written and directed by james cameron

thanks to michu and jackie, la chaussee, france

Indigo Dreams Publishing Ltd
24, Forest Houses
Cookworthy Moor
Halwill
Beaworthy
Devon
EX21 5UU
www.indigodreams.co.uk